THE GREAT PESHTIGO FIRE

THE GREAT PESHTIGO FIRE
AN EYEWITNESS ACCOUNT

BY REVEREND PETER PERNIN

SECOND EDITION

WITH A FOREWORD BY STEPHEN J. PYNE

INTRODUCTION AND EPILOGUE BY
WILLIAM CONVERSE HAYGOOD

STATE HISTORICAL SOCIETY OF WISCONSIN
MADISON
1999

The editors gratefully acknowledge the several individuals whose
contributions greatly enhance this new edition. Our thanks go to Rosemary
Reed for her contemporary photograph of Malibu; to the Mayor of Peshtigo,
Dale Berman, and the many local historians in Peshtigo who assisted us with
information. We especially thank proofreader Ellen Goldlust-Gingrich,
cartographer Jeff Maas, who provided us with updated maps, and Jill
Bremigan, our excellent book designer and artist. Their work guarantees a
superior publication.

On the cover: *Detail from artist Mel Kishner's depiction of villagers fleeing down
Oconto Avenue. WHi (X3) 35248*

Library of Congress Cataloging-in-Publication Data

Pernin, Peter, 19th cent.
     The great Peshtigo fire: an eyewitness account /by Peter Pernin; with a
foreword by Stephen J. Pyne and an introduction by William C. Haygood. --
2nd ed.
     ISBN 0-87020-310-X (paper)
     1. Peshtigo Region (Wis.)--History--19th century. 2. Forest fires--
Wisconsin--Peshtigo Region--History--19th century. I. State Historical Society
of Wisconsin. II. Title.
     F589.P48P47   1999
     977.5'33--dc21
                                                                    99-27393
                                                                    CIP

❧CONTENTS❧

MAPS

THE PESHTIGO PARADIGM

BY STEPHEN J. PYNE

America's "forgotten fire" is anything but. It burned deeply into regional memory, its roster of dead qualifies it as one of the greatest quasi-natural disasters in North America, it springs from the pages of every survey of American fires, and its cachet as "forgotten" has paradoxically helped make it better known than almost any other rural conflagration, even the much larger Miramichi (northeast New Brunswick, 1825) and North Carolina (1898) fires. The holocaust that history knows as the Peshtigo Fire has never long passed from our national consciousness. In truth, the fire is one of a handful recognized generally throughout the world.

But these are far from the only reasons to recall it now. The firestorm's meaning—call it the Peshtigo paradigm—endures. The conflagration of October 8, 1871, illustrated a formula for forest fire disaster that has proved timeless. Its ravages contributed to a philosophy of conservation that has informed fire programs over the last century. And its descendant avatars flare today in Amazonia and Borneo, in California and Florida, and in the image of fire as the specter of ecological apocalypse. The fires of 1871 are not merely a historic relic: their story continues to be retold and deserves to be remembered.

What we call the "Peshtigo Fire" is a code name for a vast landscape of burning. The event raged within a regional complex that splashed across some 2,400 square miles and engulfed even Chicago. A prolonged drought, a rural agriculture based on burning, railroads that cast sparks to all sides, a landscape stuffed with slash and debris from logging, a city built largely of forest materials, the catalytic passage of a dry cold front—all ensured that fires would break out, that some would become monumental, that flames would swallow wooden villages and metropolitan blocks with equal aplomb. Far from diminishing the horrors of Peshtigo, the Chicago conflagration ensured that what happened in frontier Wisconsin would be recorded. Here was fire's contribution to what environmental historian William

Cronon has called "Nature's Metropolis"—Chicago. Here was the grisly reality to match the metaphor coined for the post-Civil War era by Vernon Louis Parrington—the "Great Barbecue."

That domain of fire extended through time as well. When railroads punched into the North Woods after the Civil War, they set off a shock wave whose fiery aftertremors continued until the 1930s, when a combination of ecological exhaustion, economic conversion, and state intervention finally throttled routine wildfire from the land. These circumstances were not unique to the United States. Similar fires erupted along all of Europe's colonial frontiers. They incinerated logging communities in northern Sweden; they pounced on Russian villages along the flanks of the Trans-Siberian railway; they gutted New Zealand's North Island in 1885; they burned Gippsland, Australia, during the 1898 "Red Tuesday" fires; they blasted wooden towns in turn-of-the-century British Columbia and 1910s Ontario. Large fires were as characteristic of brash, relentless frontiers as wooden shacks and mud roads.

What happened in Peshtigo, Wisconsin, on October 8, 1871, was part of a ring of fire that continues to ripple around the globe. Analogous flames occur today. Substitute Xilinji and Ma Lin in Manchuria for Hinckley and Cloquet in Minnesota, and you have the Great Black Dragon fire that gutted three million acres in 1987 in Manchuria, devoured several rail-and-logging communities, killed hundreds, and left 33,706 homeless. The dynamics of wholesale land conversion in Amazonia, Borneo, and Sumatra that have so appalled contemporary environmentalists and have smothered Southeast Asia in smoke are exactly those that burned out the North Woods and forced lighthouses into action in midday along the shores of the Great Lakes. America was then a developing nation; it displayed the fire practices characteristic of one. If you want to understand why such immense areas are burning today—why they seem so intractable—you need only reconsider the Peshtigo paradigm and recall how stubbornly that fatal formula persisted in Wisconsin, Michigan, and Minnesota, well beyond the time when the United States considered itself an urban nation and a leading industrial power.

Again like modern fires, those of the late nineteenth century attracted critics and sparked calls for reform. Charred bodies, seared towns, and organic soils burned to sand were not inducements for further settlement, the investment capital of future wealth, or the signatures of a civilized people. Such fires argued for an emerging philosophy of conservation in ways that the subtle tracking of soil erosion or protests over killing of flamingos could not. The lethal burns shouted the inadequacy of laissez-faire settlement by ordinary folk. Gilded Age America was the burning Brazil of its day. Years later, when Aldo Leopold elaborated his ideas on land ethics and stewardship, he included the 1871 fires as an environmental milepost. His *Sand County Almanac* (1949) derived from a site logged, burned, and abandoned—a synecdoche for the regional havoc that Peshtigo so aptly symbolized.

The actual reforms emerged elsewhere. The creation of public lands, particularly national forests, was intended to prevent the wholesale wastage that had so pillaged the North Woods. The immediate prods for federal fire protection, especially, were the 1903 and 1908 fires in the Northeast and the 1902 and 1910 fires in the Northwest. But behind them stood the memory of Peshtigo. The creation of a forestry establishment, in turn, helped dampen the fury of the rural fire scene. Peshtigo rose from the ashes. Eventually, tree farms replaced stump farms, the woods were reseeded, tourists succeeded transient loggers, fields regrew as summer home sites. And the fires returned.

This return betrays more than a regional anomaly. It advertises a pattern that had become transnational. Throughout the industrial world, a rural landscape, generally depressed economically, often abandoned, is being recolonized by exurbanites. In some places fragments of cities have sprawled into woods, in others the woods have overgrown houses. The wild and the urban have met, mingled, and too often melted. By 1990, intermix rural-urban fires had become the defining fire problem of the United States. But fires around Sydney, Athens, and Provence show that modern colonization has a characteristic fire frontier that, like its rural predecessor, is encircling Earth.

A revised formula for settlement, founded on twentieth-century suburbs and fire exclusion, has replaced the old nineteenth-century formula grounded in farms and fire use. The scene has eerily inverted, like an image projected through a crystal point. So while it seems inappropriate to equate Peshtigo and its tragic loss of life with the modern fires in Malibu, California, and Flagler County, Florida, the ecological and social dynamics of their burning are mirror images. Fuels build up not because the woods are cut but because they aren't. Wildfires burn fiercely not because controlled burns escape but because no other kind of fire is allowed. Urban values that denounce all smoke as pollution replace rural values that had viewed smoke as an engine of progress. A misreading of the Peshtigo legacy—that fire abolition was the answer to fire abuse—threatens to recreate the old burn in more modern idiom. So, in especially ironic inversion, environmentalists have found themselves arguing that fire ought to be put back into the land rather than be extirpated from it. Restored fire has come to be a symbol of renewed land stewardship.

All this has expanded and revived the Peshtigo paradigm. Peshtigo perished because of poor practices and poor timing both, not because logging was inevitably fatal, the town recklessly located, and fire itself intrinsically bad. Without good fires Peshtigo could not have existed

The ruins of Peshtigo and a small group of fire survivors (left), 1871.

(and not to have used fire at all is to use it badly). Like all classics, the fire invites close, nuanced reading and rereading because its story lives. The firestorm that engulfed a rough-settled Wisconsin in 1871 continues to lurk in the virtual wilds of exurban America and in much else of an unsettled Earth. The next time a smoke pall immerses Singapore, flames overrun suburbs along the San Gabriel Mountains, an escaped pasture fire levels Trans-Baikalian villages in the Russian Federation, fallow burning leaps into a Ghanaian cocoa plantation, or a conflagration incinerates summer homes along the Mogollon Rim in Arizona (its long-unburned pines thick as the quills on a porcupine's back), observers could do worse than to reexamine the Peshtigo paradigm. And for that task there is no better introduction than Father Peter Pernin's riveting narrative.

Tempe, Arizona
1999

Malibu, California, November of 1993, and the effects of a Peshtigo-like firestorm.

❧INTRODUCTION❧

BY WILLIAM CONVERSE HAYGOOD

On October 8, 1871, two of the greatest natural catastrophes in the history of the Middle West occurred. Ironically, both happened not only on the same day but almost at the same hour; both had been preceded by ample but disregarded omens; and both stemmed from the same fundamental causes—wood rendered tinder-dry by prolonged drought, plus the factor of human carelessness. In Chicago, a lantern thoughtlessly placed within kicking distance of a cow in a barn on De Koven Street is reputed to have set off the most destructive metropolitan blaze in the nation's history, resulting in property damage of $200,000,000 and virtually annihilating the city's core. In northeastern Wisconsin, fires set by hunters, lumberjacks, railroad workers and locomotives, and farmers burning stumps and rubble culminated in the nation's worst forest fire in terms of lives lost.

Although the Wisconsin fire ravaged 2,400 square miles and destroyed numerous settlements and isolated farms on both sides of Green Bay, it has gone down in history as the Peshtigo fire, because it was in this village and in the farming area immediately surrounding it that industry and population were the most concentrated, that the fire reached its greatest virulence, and that the majority of the fatalities occurred.

In the fall of 1871, like other localities to which the expanding railroads were bringing an undreamed prosperity, Peshtigo, on the river of the same name in Marinette County, was exploiting the surrounding forest lands to the fullest advantage. William G. Ogden, the Chicago millionaire, had invested heavily in what was then the country's largest woodenware factory to convert the river-borne logs into such articles as pails, tubs, broom handles, barrel covers, and clothespins. There were also a sawmill; a sash, door, and blind factory; a foundry and blacksmith shop; stores, hotels, and a boardinghouse; and, to the villagers' considerable pride, a schoolhouse, and a Protestant as well as a Catholic church.

All this was as of the early evening of October 8, when the village's official population of 1,700 was swollen by an influx of recently arrived laborers to work on the railroad right-of-way, in addition to the usual number of salesmen, travelers, and visitors to be found in any similar village. By daylight fewer than 1,000 of this number were still alive, and only one structure, a partially constructed house, remained standing.

Only since the 1970s have the occurrences of that dreadful night been accorded their proper place in the history of American disasters, primarily because Chicago's ordeal was by its very nature more spectacular, more universally publicized, and more often revived in print. Peshtigo's chief historians have been two journalists and a novelist. In 1871, Frank Tilton, a Green Bay newspaperman, put together a book of eyewitness accounts and his own reportage to sell for the benefit of the survivors. In 1968, Robert W. Wells of the *Milwaukee Journal* gave the Peshtigo story a skillful and readable reconstruction. In 1957, William F. Steuber, Jr., used the tragedy as the basis for a prizewinning novel, *The Landlooker*.

But no writer has yet to equal in vividness, imagery, or sheer drama the contemporary account written by Father Peter Pernin, the parish priest for Peshtigo and nearby Marinette, whose churches burned to the ground. Published in Montreal in 1874, ostensibly to raise funds for a new church in Marinette, Father Pernin's account may have also been an attempt to exorcize the memories of that October night during which he suffered fearfully while behaving heroically.

Not a great deal is known about Peter Pernin except that he was born in France about 1825 and served parishes in L'Erable and Clifton in Illinois from 1865 to 1869. He was a parish priest in Oconto in 1870 and in Marinette from 1871 to 1874. From 1876 to 1878 he was at Grand Rapids (Wisconsin Rapids), and in 1879 he was at La Crescent, Minnesota, in which state he continued to serve a number of parishes, the last recorded one being in 1898, when he was at St. Joseph's Church in Rushmore, Diocese of Winona.

In 1918–1919 Joseph Schafer serialized parts of Father Pernin's account in the *Wisconsin Magazine of History* (vol. 2). In reprinting it we have added some material that Mr. Schafer omitted and have supplied endnotes wherever they seemed necessary to further clarify the events described.

Madison, Wisconsin
1971

Before the fire. Peshtigo bird's-eye of 1871.

❧AN EYEWITNESS ACCOUNT❧

BY REVEREND PETER PERNIN

A country covered with dense forests, in the midst of which are to be met with here and there, along newly opened roads, clearings of more or less extent, sometimes a half league in width to afford space for an infant town, or perhaps three or four acres intended for a farm. With the exception of these isolated spots where the trees have been cut down and burned, all is a wild but majestic forest. Trees, trees everywhere, nothing else but trees as far as you can travel from the bay, either towards the north or west. These immense forests are bounded on the east by Green Bay of Lake Michigan, and by the lake itself.

The face of the country is in general undulating, diversified by valleys overgrown with cedars and spruce trees, sandy hills covered with evergreens, and large tracts of rich land filled with the different varieties of hard wood, oak, maple, beech, ash, elm, and birch. The climate of this region is generally uniform and favorable to the crops that are now tried there with remarkable success. Rains are frequent, and they generally fall at a favorable time.

15

The year 1871 was, however, distinguished by its unusual dryness. Farmers had profited of the latter circumstance to enlarge their clearings, cutting down and burning the wood that stood in their way. Hundreds of laborers employed in the construction of a railroad had acted in like manner, availing themselves of both axe and fire to advance their work. Hunters and Indians scour these forests continually, especially in the autumn season, at which time they ascend the streams for trout-fishing, or disperse through the woods deer-stalking. At night they kindle a large fire wherever they may chance to halt, prepare their suppers, then wrapping themselves in their blankets, sleep peacefully, extended on the earth, knowing that the fire will keep at a distance any wild animals that may happen to range through the vicinity during the night. The ensuing morning they depart without taking the precaution of extinguishing the smouldering embers of the fire that has protected and warmed them. Farmers and others act in a similar manner. In this way the woods, particularly in the fall, are gleaming everywhere with fires lighted by man, and which, fed on every side by dry leaves and branches, spread more or less. If fanned by a brisk gale of wind they are liable to assume most formidable proportions.

Twice or thrice before October 8, the effects of the wind, favored by the general dryness, had filled the inhabitants of the environs with consternation. A few details on this point may interest the reader, and serve at the same time to illustrate more fully the great catastrophe which overwhelmed us later. The destructive element seemed whilst multiplying its warning to be at the same time essaying its own strength. On September 22 I was summoned, in the exercise of my ministry, to the Sugar Bush,[1] a place in the neighborhood of Peshtigo, where a number of farms lie adjacent to each other. Whilst waiting at one of these, isolated from the rest, I took a gun, and, accompanied by a lad of twelve years of age, who offered to guide me through the wood, started in pursuit of some of the pheasants which abounded in the environs. At the expiration of a few hours, seeing that the sun was sinking in the horizon, I bade the child reconduct me to the farmhouse. He endeavored to do so but without success. We went on and on, now turning to the right, now to the left, but without coming in view of our destination. In less than a half hour's wanderings we perceived that we were completely lost in the woods. Night was setting in, and nature was silently preparing for the season of rest. The only sounds audible were the crackling of a tiny tongue of fire that ran along the ground, in and out, among the trunks of the trees, leaving them unscathed but devouring the dry leaves that came in its way, and the swaying of the upper branches of the trees announcing that the wind was rising. We shouted loudly, but without evoking any reply. I then fired off my gun several times as tokens of distress. Finally a distant halloo reached our ears, then another, then several coming from different directions. Rendered anxious by our prolonged absence, the parents of my companion and the farm servants had finally suspected the truth and set out to seek us. Directed to our quarter by our shouts and the firing, they were soon on the right road when a new obstacle presented itself. Fanned by the wind, the tiny flames previously mentioned had united and spread over a considerable surface. We thus found ourselves in the center of a circle of fire extending or narrowing, more or less, around us. We could not reach the men who had come to our assistance, nor could we go to them without incurring the risk of seriously scorching our feet or of being suffocated by the smoke. They were obliged to fray a passage for us by beating the fire with branches of trees at one particular point, thus momentarily staying its progress whilst we rapidly made our escape.

The danger proved more imminent in places exposed to the wind, and I learned the following day, on my return to Peshtigo, that the town had been in great peril at the very time that I had lost myself in the woods. The wind had risen, and, fanning the flames, had driven them in the direction of the houses. Hogsheads of water were placed at intervals all round the town, ready for any emergency.

I will now mention another incident that happened a few days before the great catastrophe:

I was driving homeward after having visited my second parish situated on the banks of the River Menominee, about two leagues distant.[2] Whilst quietly following the public road opened through the forest, I remarked little fires gleaming here and there along the route, sometimes on one side, sometimes on the other. Suddenly I arrived at a spot where the flames were burning on both sides at once with more violence than elsewhere. The smoke, driven to the front, filled the road and obscured it to such a degree that I could neither see the extent of the fire nor judge the amount of danger. I inferred, however, that the latter was not very great as the wind was not against me. I

17

WHi (X3) 24395

Reverend Peter Pernin, about 1874.

entered then, though at first hesitatingly, into the dense cloud of smoke left darkling behind by the flames burning fiercely forward. My horse hung back, but I finally succeeded in urging him on, and in five or six minutes we emerged safely from this labyrinth of fire and smoke. Here we found ourselves confronted by a dozen vehicles arrested in their course by the conflagration.

"Can we pass?" inquired one.

"Yes, since I have just done so, but loosen your reins and urge on your horse or you may be suffocated."

Some of the number dashed forward, others had not the hardihood to follow, and consequently returned to Peshtigo.

🔥🔥🔥🔥🔥

IT MAY THUS BE SEEN THAT WARNINGS WERE NOT WANTING. I give now another trait, more striking than either of those just related, copied from a journal published at Green Bay.[3] It is a description of a combat sustained against the terrible element of fire at Peshtigo, Sunday, September 24, just two weeks before the destruction of the village:

> Sunday, the 24th inst., was an exciting, I might say a fearful time, in Peshtigo. For several days the fires had been raging in the timber all around—north, south, east and west. Saturday the flames burned through to the river a little above the town; and on Saturday night, much danger was apprehended from the sparks and cinders that blew across the river, into the upper part of the town, near the factory. A force was stationed along the river, and although fire caught in the sawdust and dry slabs it was promptly extinguished. It was a grand sight, the fire that night. It burned to the tops of the tallest trees, enveloped them in a mantle of flames, or, winding itself about them like a huge serpent, crept to their summits, out upon the branches, and

wound its huge folds about them. Hissing and glaring it lapped out its myriad fiery tongues while its fierce breath swept off the green leaves and roared through the forest like a tempest. Ever and anon some tall old pine, whose huge trunk had become a column of fire, fell with a thundering crash, filling the air with an ascending cloud of sparks and cinders, whilst above this sheet of flames a dense black cloud of resinous smoke, in its strong contrast to the light beneath, seemed to threaten death and destruction to all below.

Thousands of birds, driven from their roosts, flew about as if uncertain which way to go, and made the night still more hideous by their startled cries. Frequently they would fly hither and thither, calling loudly for their mates, then, hovering for a moment in the air, suddenly dart downward and disappear in the fiery furnace beneath. Thus the night wore away while all earnestly hoped, and many hearts fervently prayed for rain.

Sunday morning the fires had died down so that we began to hope the danger was over. About eleven o'clock, while the different congregations were assembled in their respective churches, the steam whistle of the factory blew a wild blast of alarm. In a moment the temples were emptied of their worshippers, the latter rushing wildly out to see what had happened. Fire had caught in the sawdust near the factory again, but before we reached the spot it was extinguished. The wind had suddenly risen and was blowing a gale from the northwest. The fires in the timber were burning more fiercely than ever, and were approaching the river directly opposite the factory. The air was literally filled with the burning coals and cinders, which fell, setting fire all around, and the utmost diligence was necessary to prevent these flames from spreading. The engine was brought out, and hundreds of pails from the factory were manned; in short, everything that was possible was done to prevent the fire from entering the town.

But now a new danger arose. The fires to the west of the town were approaching rapidly, and it seemed that

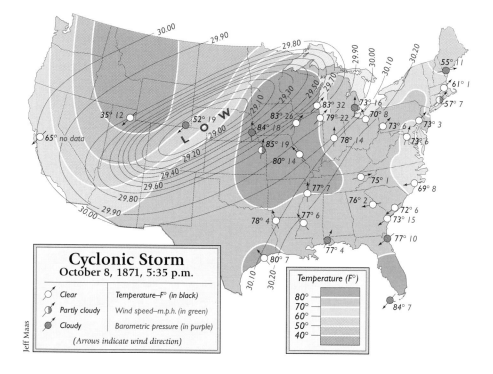

Cyclonic Storm
October 8, 1871, 5:35 p.m.

○ Clear	Temperature–F° (in black)
◐ Partly cloudy	Wind speed—m.p.h. (in green)
● Cloudy	Barometric pressure (in purple)
(Arrows indicate wind direction)	

Temperature (F°)

80°
70°
60°
50°
40°

Jeff Maas

nothing short of a miracle could save it from utter destruction. A cloud of hot, blinding smoke blew in our faces and made it extremely difficult to see or do anything; still prompt and energetic means were taken to check the approaching flames.

The Company's teams were set to carrying water, and the whole force of over three hundred of the laborers in the factory and mills were on the ground, besides other citizens. Goods were packed up, and moved from buildings supposed to be in immediate danger. Indeed a general conflagration seemed inevitable. I have seen fires sweep over the prairies with the speed of a locomotive, and the prairie fire is grand and terrific; but beside a timber fire it sinks into insignificance. In proportion as the timber is denser, heavier, and loftier than the prairie grass, the timber fire is intenser, hotter, grander, than the prairie fire. The fire on the prairie before a high wind will rush on and lap up the light dead grass, and it is gone in a breath. In the timber it may move almost as rapidly, but the fire does not go out with the advance waves which sweep over the tops of the trees and catch the light limbs and foliage. Nor is there the same chance to resist the approach of fire in the forests. It is as though you attempted to resist the approach of an avalanche of fire hurled against you. With the going down of the sun the wind abated and with it the fire. Timber was felled and water thrown over it; buildings were covered with wet blankets and all under the scorching heat and in blinding suffocating smoke that was enough to strangle one, and thus passed the night of Sunday.

Monday, the wind veered to the south, and cleared away the smoke. Strange to say not a building was burned—the town was saved. Monday the factory was closed to give the men rest, and today, September 27, all is quiet and going on as usual.

What did these repeated alarms filling the minds of the people with anxiety during the three or four weeks preceding the great calamity seem to indicate!

Doubtless they might have been looked on as the natural results of the great dryness, the number of fires lighted throughout the forests by hunters or others, as well as of the wind that fanned from time to time these fires, augmenting their strength and volume, but who will dare to say that they were not specially ordained by Him who is master of causes as well as of their effects? Does He not in most cases avail Himself of natural causes to execute His will and bring about the most wonderful results? It would indeed be difficult for anyone who had assisted as I had done at the terrible events following so closely on the above mentioned indications not to see in them the hand of God, and infer in consequence that these various signs were but forerunners of the great tragedy for which He wished us to be in some degree prepared.

I cannot say whether they were looked on by many in this light or not, but certainly some were greatly alarmed and prepared as far as lay in their power for a general conflagration, burying in the earth those objects which they specially wished to save. The Company caused all combustible materials on which a fire could possibly feed to be taken away, and augmented the number of water hogsheads girdling the town. Wise precautions certainly, which could have been of great service in any ordinary case of fire but which were utterly unavailing in the awful conflagration that burst upon us. They served nevertheless to demonstrate more clearly the *finger of God* in the events which succeeded.

"Queen" Marinette and her home, one of the first built in the Peshtigo area.

As for myself, I allowed things to take their course without feeling any great anxiety as to consequences, or taking any precautionary steps, a frame of mind very different to that which I was destined to experience on the evening of the eighth of October.

A word now about my two parishes.

Peshtigo is situated on a river of that name, about six miles from Green Bay with which it communicates by means of a small railroad. The Company established at Peshtigo is a source of prosperity to the whole country, not only from its spirit of enterprise and large pecuniary resources but also from its numerous establishments, the most important of which, a factory of tubs and buckets, affords alone steady employment to more than three hundred workmen. The population of Peshtigo, including the farmers settled in the neighborhood, numbered then about two thousand souls. We were just finishing the construction of a church looked on as a great embellishment to the parish.

My abode was near the church, to the west of the river, and about a five or six minute walk from the latter. I mention this so as to render the circumstances of my escape through the midst of the flames more intelligible.

Besides Peshtigo, I had the charge of another parish much more important situated on the River Menominee, at the point where it empties into Green Bay. It is called Marinette, from a female half breed, looked on as their queen by the Indians inhabiting that district. This woman received in baptism the name of Mary, *Marie*, which subsequently was corrupted into that of Marinette, or little Marie. Hence the name of Marinette bestowed on the place. It is there that we are at present building a church in honor of our Lady of Lourdes. At the time of the fire, Marinette possessed a church, a handsome new presbytery just finished, in which I was on the point of taking up my abode, besides a house in course of construction, destined to serve as a parish school.

The population was about double that of Peshtigo.

Before entering into details, I will mention one more circumstance which may appear providential in the eyes of some, though brought about by purely natural causes.

At the time of the catastrophe our church at Peshtigo was ready for plastering, the ensuing Monday being appointed for commencing the work. The lime and marble dust were lying ready in front of the building, whilst the altar and various ornaments, as well as the pews, had all been removed. Being unable in consequence to officiate that Sunday in the sacred edifice, I told the people that there would be no mass, notifying at the same time the Catholics of Cedar River that I would spend the Sunday among them. The latter place was another of my missions, situated on Green Bay, four or five leagues north of Marinette. Saturday then, October 7, in accordance with my promise, I left Peshtigo and proceeded to the Menominee wharf to take passage on the steamboat *Dunlap*. There I vainly waited her coming several hours. It was the only time that year she had failed in the regularity of her trips. I learned after that the steamboat had passed as usual but stood out from shore, not deeming it prudent to approach nearer. The temperature was low, and the sky obscured by a dense mass of smoke which no breath of wind arose to dispel, a circumstance rendering navigation very dangerous especially in the neighborhood of the shore.[4] Towards nightfall, when all hope of embarking was over, I returned to Peshtigo on horseback. After informing the people that mass would be said in my own abode the following morning, I prepared a temporary altar in one of the rooms, employing for the purpose the tabernacle itself which I had taken from the church, and after mass I replaced the Blessed Sacrament in it, intending to say mass again there the next Monday.

In the afternoon, when about leaving for Marinette where I was accustomed to chant vespers and preach when high mass was said at Peshtigo, which was every fortnight, my departure was strongly opposed by several of my parishioners. There seemed to be a vague fear of some impending though unknown evil haunting the minds of many, nor was I myself entirely free from this unusual feeling. It was rather an impression than a conviction, for, on reflecting, I saw that things looked much as usual, and arrived at the conclusion that our fears were groundless, without, however, feeling much reassured thereby.

WHi (X3) 24401

A wood engraving of the Peshtigo Congregational Church in 1871.

But for the certainty that the Catholics at Marinette, supposing me at Cedar River, would not, consequently, come to vespers, I would probably have persisted in going there, but under actual circumstances I deemed it best to yield to the representations made me and remain where I was.

God willed that I should be at the post of danger. The steamboat which I had expected to bear me from Peshtigo, on the seventh of October, had of course obeyed the elements which prevented her landing, but God is the master of these elements and Him they obey. Thus I found myself at Peshtigo Sunday evening, October 8, where, according to all previous calculations, projects, and arrangements, I should not have been.

The afternoon passed in complete inactivity. I remained still a prey to the indefinable apprehensions of impending calamity already alluded to, apprehensions contradicted by reason which assured me there was no more cause for present fear than there had been eight or fifteen days before—indeed less, on account of the precautions taken and the numerous sentinels watching over the public safety. These two opposite sentiments, one of which persistently asserted itself despite every effort to shake it off, whilst the other, inspired by reason was powerless to reassure me, plunged my faculties into a species of mental torpor.

In the outer world everything contributed to keep alive these two different impressions. On one side, the thick smoke darkening the sky, the heavy, suffocating atmosphere, the mysterious silence filling the air, so often a presage of storm, seemed to afford grounds for fear in case of a sudden gale. On the other hand the passing and repassing in the street of countless young people bent only on amusement, laughing, singing, and perfectly indifferent to the menacing aspect of nature, was sufficient to make me think that I alone was a prey to anxiety, and to render me ashamed of manifesting the feeling.

During the afternoon, an old Canadian, remarkable for the deep interest he always took in everything relating to the church, came and asked permission to dig a well close to the sacred edifice so as to have water ready at hand in case of accident, as well as for the use of the plasterer who was coming to work the following morning. As my petitioner had no time to devote to the task during the course of the week, I assented. His labor completed, he informed me there was abundance of water, adding with an expression of deep satisfaction: "Father, not for a large sum of money would I give that well. Now if a fire breaks out again it will be easy to save our church." As he seemed greatly fatigued, I made him partake of supper and then sent him to rest. An hour after he was buried in deep slumber, but God was watching over him, and to reward him doubtless for the zeal he had displayed for the interests of his Father's House, enabled the pious old man to save his life; whilst in the very building in which he had been sleeping more than fifty people, fully awake, perished.

What we do for God is never lost, even in this world.

Towards seven in the evening, always haunted by the same

misgivings, I left home to see how it went with my neighbors. I stepped over first to the house of an elderly kind-hearted widow, a Mrs. Dress, and we walked out together on her land. The wind was beginning to rise, blowing in short fitful gusts as if to try its strength and then as quickly subsiding. My companion was as troubled as myself, and kept pressing her children to take some precautionary measures, but they refused, laughing lightly at her fears. At one time, whilst we were still in the fields, the wind rose suddenly with more strength than it had yet displayed and I perceived some old trunks of trees blaze out though without seeing about them any tokens of cinder or spark, just as if the wind had been a breath of fire, capable of kindling them into a flame by its mere contact. We extinguished these; the wind fell again, and nature resumed her moody and mysterious silence. I re-entered the house but only to leave it, feeling restless, though at the same time devoid of anything like energy, and retraced my steps to my own abode to conceal within it as I best could my vague but continually deepening anxieties. On looking towards the west, whence the wind had persistently blown for hours past, I perceived above the dense cloud of smoke over-hanging the earth, a vivid red reflection of immense extent, and then suddenly struck on my ear, strangely audible in the preternatural silence reigning around, a distant roaring, yet muffled sound, announcing that the elements were in commotion somewhere. I rapidly resolved to return home and prepare, without further hesitation, for whatever events were impending. From listless and undecided as I had previously been, I suddenly became active and determined. This change of mind was a great relief. The vague fears that had heretofore pursued me vanished, and another idea, certainly not a result of anything like mental reasoning on my part, took possession of my mind; it was, not to lose much time in saving my effects but to direct my flight as speedily as possible in the direction of the river. Henceforth this became my ruling thought, and it was entirely unaccompanied by anything like fear or perplexity. My mind seemed all at once to become perfectly tranquil.

🔥🔥🔥🔥🔥

IT WAS NOW ABOUT HALF PAST EIGHT IN THE EVENING.
I first thought of my horse and turned him free into the street,
deeming that, in any case, he would have more chance of escape thus
than tied up in the stable. I then set about digging a trench six feet
wide and six or seven feet deep, in the sandy soil of the garden, and
though the earth was easy enough to work my task proved a tedious
one. The atmosphere was heavy and oppressive, strangely affecting the
strength and rendering respiration painful and laborious. The only
consideration that could have induced me to keep on working when I
found it almost impossible to move my limbs, was the fear, growing
more strongly each moment into a certainty, that some great
catastrophe was approaching. The crimson reflection in the western
portion of the sky was rapidly increasing in size and in intensity; then
between each stroke of my pickax I heard plainly, in the midst of the
unnatural calm and silence reigning around, the strange and terrible
noise already described, the muttered thunder of which became more
distinct as it drew each moment nearer. This sound resembled the
confused noise of a number of cars and locomotives approaching a
railroad station, or the rumbling of thunder, with the difference that it
never ceased, but deepened in intensity each moment more and more.
The spectacle of this menacing crimson in the sky, the sound of this
strange and unknown voice of nature constantly augmenting in
terrible majesty, seemed to endow me with supernatural strength.
Whilst toiling thus steadfastly at my task, the sound of human voices
plainly audible amid the silence and species of stupor reigning around
fell on my ear. They betrayed on the one hand thoughtlessness, on the
other folly.

A neighboring American family were entertaining some friends at
tea. The room which they occupied at the moment overlooked my
garden; thus they could see me whilst I could as easily overhear them.
More than once, the smothered laughter of some of the guests,
especially of the young girls, fell on my ear. Doubtless they were
amusing themselves at my expense. About nine, the company
dispersed, and Mrs. Tyler, the hostess, approached me. The actions of
the priest always make a certain impression, even on Protestants.

"Father," she questioned, "do you think there is any danger?"

"I do not know," was my reply, "but I have unpleasant

A wood engraving of the Peshtigo schoolhouse before the fire.

presentiments, and feel myself impelled to prepare for trouble."

"But if a fire breaks out, Father, what are we to do?"

"In that case, Madam, seek the river at once."

I gave her no reason for advising such a course, perhaps I had really none to offer, beyond that it was my innate conviction.

Shortly after, Mrs. Tyler and her family started in the direction of the river and were all saved. I learned later that out of the eight guests assembled at her house that evening, all perished with the exception of two.

At a short distance from home, on the other side of the street, was a tavern. This place had been crowded all day with revellers, about two hundred young men having arrived that Sunday morning at Peshtigo by the boat to work on the railroad.[5] Many were scattered throughout the town, where they had met acquaintances, while a large number were lodging at the tavern just mentioned. Perhaps they had passed the holy time of mass drinking and carousing there. Towards nightfall the greater part of them were too much intoxicated to take any share in the anxiety felt by the more steady members of the community, or even to notice the strange aspect of nature. Whilst working in my garden, I saw several of them hanging about the veranda of the tavern or lounging in the yard. Their intoxicated condition was plainly

28

revealed by the manner in which they quarrelled, wrestled, rolled on the ground, filling the air the while with wild shouts and horrid blasphemies.

When hastening through the street, on my way to the river at the moment the storm burst forth, the wind impelled me in the direction of this house. A death-like silence now reigned within it, as if reason had been restored to the inmates, or fear had suddenly penetrated to their hearts. Without shout or word they re-entered the place, closing the doors as if to bar death out—a few minutes later the house was swept away. What became of them I know not.

After finishing the digging of the trench I placed within it my trunks, books, church ornaments, and other valuables, covering the whole with sand to a depth of about a foot. Whilst still engaged at this, my servant, who had collected in a basket several precious objects in silver committed to my charge, such as crosses, medals, rosaries, etc., ran and deposited them on the steps of a neighboring store, scarcely conscious in her trouble of what she was doing.

She hastily returned for a cage containing her canary, which the wind, however, almost immediately tore from her grasp—and breathless with haste and terror she called to me to leave the garden and fly. The wind, forerunner of the tempest, was increasing in violence, the redness in the sky deepening, and the roaring sound like thunder seemed almost upon us. It was now time to think of the Blessed Sacrament—object of all objects, precious, priceless, especially in the eyes of a priest. It had never been a moment absent from my thoughts, for of course I had intended from the first to bring it with me. Hastening then to the chamber containing the tabernacle, I proceeded to open the latter, but the key, owing to my haste, slipped from my fingers and fell. There was no time for farther delay, so I caught up the tabernacle with its contents and carried it out, placing it in my wagon as I knew it would be much easier to draw it thus than to bear it in my arms. My thought was that I should meet someone who would help me in the task. I re-entered to seek the chalice which had not been placed in the tabernacle, when a strange and startling phenomenon met my view. It was that of a cloud of sparks that blazed up here and there with a sharp detonating sound like that of powder exploding, and flew from room to room. I understood then that the air was saturated with some special gas, and I could not help thinking if this gas lighted up from mere contact with the breath of hot wind, what would it be when fire would come in actual contact with it. The circumstance, though menacing enough, inspired me with no fear, my safety seemed already assured. Outside the door, in a cage attached to the wall, was a jay that I had had in my possession for a long time. The instinct of birds in foreseeing a storm is well known, and my poor jay was fluttering wildly round his cage, beating against its bars as if seeking to escape, and uttering shrill notes of alarm. I grieved for its fate but could do nothing for it. The lamps were burning on the table, and I thought, as I turned away, how soon their gleam would be eclipsed in the vivid light of a terrible conflagration.

I look on the peculiar, indeed almost childish frame of mind in which I then found myself, as most providential. It kept up my courage in the ordeal through which I was about to pass, veiling from me in great part its horror and danger. Any other mental condition, though perhaps more in keeping with my actual position would have paralyzed my strength and sealed my fate.

I vainly called my dog who, disobeying the summons, concealed himself under my bed, only to meet death there later. Then I hastened out to open the gate so as to bring forth my wagon. Barely had I laid hand on it, when the wind heretofore violent rose suddenly to a hurricane, and quick as lightning opened the way for my egress from the yard by sweeping planks, gate, and fencing away into space. "The road is open," I thought, "we have only to start."

I had delayed my departure too long. It would be impossible to describe the trouble I had to keep my feet, to breathe, to retain hold of the buggy which the wind strove to tear from my grasp, or to keep the tabernacle in its place. To reach the river, even unencumbered by any charge, was more than many succeeded in doing; several failed, perishing in the attempt. How I arrived at it is even to this day a mystery to myself.

The air was no longer fit to breathe, full as it was of sand, dust, ashes, cinders, sparks, smoke, and fire. It was almost impossible to keep one's eyes unclosed, to distinguish the road, or to recognize people, though the way was crowded with pedestrians, as well as vehicles crossing and crashing against each other in the general flight. Some were hastening towards the river, others from it, whilst all were struggling alike in the grasp of the hurricane. A thousand discordant deafening noises rose on the air together. The neighing of horses, falling of chimneys, crashing of uprooted trees, roaring and whistling of the wind, crackling of fire as it ran with lightning-like rapidity from house to house—all sounds were there save that of the human voice. People seemed stricken dumb by terror. They jostled each other without exchanging look, word, or counsel. The silence of the tomb reigned among the living; nature alone lifted up its voice and spoke. Though meeting crowded vehicles taking a direction quite opposite to that which I myself was following, it never even entered my mind that it would perhaps be better for me to follow them. Probably it was the same thing with them. We all hurried blindly on to our fate.

Almost with the first steps taken in the street the wind overturned and dragged me with the wagon close to the tavern already mentioned. Farther on, I was again thrown down over some motionless object lying on the earth; it proved to be a woman and a little girl, both dead. I raised a head that fell back heavily as lead. With a long breath I rose to my feet, but only to be hurled down again. Farther on I met my horse whom I had set free in the street. Whether he recognized me—whether he was in that spot by chance, I cannot say, but whilst struggling anew to my feet, I felt his head leaning on my shoulder. He was trembling in every limb. I called him by name and motioned him to follow me, but he did not move. He was found partly consumed by fire in the same place.

Arrived near the river, we saw that the houses adjacent to it were on fire, whilst the wind blew the flames and cinders directly into the water. The place was no longer safe. I resolved then to cross to the other side though the bridge was already on fire. The latter presented a scene of indescribable and awful confusion, each one thinking he could attain safety on the other side of the river. Those who lived in the east were hurrying towards the west, and those who dwelt in that west were wildly pushing on to the east so that the bridge was thoroughly encumbered with cattle, vehicles, women, children, and men, all pushing and crushing against each other so as to find an issue from it. Arrived amid the crowd on the other side, I resolved to descend the river, to a certain distance below the dam, where I knew the shore was lower and the water shallower, but this I found impossible. The sawmill on the same side, at the angle of the bridge, as well as the large store belonging to the Company standing opposite across the road, were both on fire. The flames from these two edifices met across the road, and none could traverse this fiery passage without meeting with instant death. I was thus obliged to ascend the

31

river on the left bank, above the dam, where the water gradually attained a great depth. After placing a certain distance between myself and the bridge, the fall of which I momentarily expected, I pushed my wagon containing the tabernacle as far into the water as possible. It was all that I could do. Henceforth I had to look to the saving of my life. The whirlwind in its continual ascension had, so to speak, worked up the smoke, dust, and cinders, so that, at least, we could see clear before us. The banks of the river as far as the eye could reach were covered with people standing there, motionless as statues, some with eyes staring, upturned towards heaven, and tongues protruded. The greater number seemed to have no idea of taking any steps to procure their safety, imagining, as many afterwards acknowledged to me, that the end of the world had arrived and that here was nothing for them but silent submission to their fate. Without uttering a word—the efforts I had made in dragging my wagon with me in my flight had left me perfectly breathless, besides the violence of the storm entirely prevented anything like speech—I pushed the persons standing on each side of me into the water. One of these sprang back again with a half smothered cry, murmuring: "I am wet"; but immersion in water was better than immersion in fire. I caught him again and dragged him out with me into the river as far as possible. At the same moment I heard a splash of the water along the river's brink. All had followed my example. It was time; the air was no longer fit for inhalation, whilst the intensity of the heat was increasing. A few minutes more and no living thing could have resisted its fiery breath.

🔥🔥🔥🔥🔥

IT WAS ABOUT TEN O'CLOCK WHEN WE ENTERED INTO the river. When doing so I neither knew the length of time we would be obliged to remain there, nor what would ultimately happen to us, yet, wonderful to relate my fate had never caused me a moment of anxiety from the time that, yielding to the involuntary impulse warning me to prepare for danger, I had resolved on directing my flight towards the river. Since then I had remained in the same careless frame of mind, which permitted me to struggle against the most insuperable obstacles, to brave the most appalling dangers, without ever seeming to remember that my life might pay the forfeit. Once in

An artist's conception of the panic at the riverside from the November 25, 1871, issue of Harper's Weekly.

water up to our necks, I thought we would, at least be safe from fire, but it was not so; the flames darted over the river as they did over land, the air was full of them, or rather the air itself was on fire. Our heads were in continual danger. It was only by throwing water constantly over them and our faces, and beating the river with our hands that we kept the flames at bay. Clothing and quilts had been thrown into the river, to save them, doubtless, and they were floating all around. I caught at some that came within reach and covered with them the heads of the persons who were leaning against or clinging to me. These wraps dried quickly in the furnace-like heat and caught fire whenever we ceased sprinkling them. The terrible whirlwind that had burst over us at the moment I was leaving home had, with its continually revolving circle of opposing winds, cleared the atmosphere. The river was as bright, brighter than by day, and the spectacle presented by these heads rising above the level of the water, some covered, some uncovered, the countless hands employed in beating the waves, was singular and painful in the extreme. So free was I from the fear and anxiety that might naturally have been expected to reign in my mind at such a moment, that I actually perceived the ludicrous side of the scene at times and smiled within myself at it. When turning my gaze from the river I chanced to look either to the right or left, before me or upwards, I saw nothing but flames; houses, trees, and the air itself were on fire. Above my head, as far as the eye could reach into space, alas! too brilliantly lighted, I saw nothing but immense volumes of flames covering the firmament, rolling one over the other with stormy violence as we see masses of clouds driven wildly hither and thither by the fierce power of the tempest.

Near me, on the bank of the river, rose the store belonging to the factory, a large three-story building, filled with tubs, buckets, and other articles. Sometimes the thought crossed my mind that if the wind happened to change, we should be buried beneath the blazing ruins of this place, but still the supposition did not cause me much apprehension. When I was entering the water, this establishment was just taking fire; the work of destruction was speedy, for, in less than a quarter of an hour, the large beams were lying blazing on the ground, while the rest of the building was either burned or swept off into space.

Not far from me a woman was supporting herself in the water by means of a log. After a time a cow swam past. There were more than a dozen of these animals in the river, impelled thither by instinct, and they succeeded in saving their lives. The first mentioned one overturned in its passage the log to which the woman was clinging and she disappeared into the water. I thought her lost; but soon saw her emerge from it holding on with one hand to the horns of the cow, and throwing water on her head with the other. How long she remained in this critical position I know not, but I was told later that the animal had swam to shore, bearing her human burden safely with her; and what threatened to bring destruction to the woman had proved the means of her salvation.

At the moment I was entering the river, another woman, terrified and breathless, reached its bank. She was leading one child by the hand, and held pressed to her breast what appeared to be another, enveloped in a roll of disordered linen, evidently caught up in haste. O horror! on opening these wraps to look on the face of her child it was not there. It must have slipped from her grasp in her hurried flight. No words could portray the look of stupor, of desolation that flitted across the poor mother's face. The half smothered cry: "Ah! my child!" escaped her, then she wildly strove to force her way through the crowd so as to cast herself into the river. The force of the wind was less violent on water than on land, and permitted the voice to be heard. I then endeavored to calm the anguish of the poor bereaved woman by suggesting that her child had been found by others and saved, but she did not even look in my direction, but stood there motionless, her eyes wild and staring, fixed on the opposite shore. I soon lost sight of her, and was informed subsequently that she had succeeded in throwing herself into the river where she met death.

Things went well enough with me during the first three or four hours of this prolonged bath, owing in part, I suppose, to my being continually in motion, either throwing water on my own head or on that of my neighbors.

It was not so, however, with some of those who were standing near me, for their teeth were chattering and their limbs convulsively trembling. Reaction was setting in and the cold penetrating through their frames. Dreading that so long a sojourn in the water might be followed by severe cramps, perhaps death, I endeavored to ascend the bank a short distance, so as to ascertain the temperature, but my shoulders were scarcely out of the river, when a voice called to me: "Father, beware, you are on fire!"

The hour of deliverance from this prison of fire and water had not yet arrived—the struggle was not yet over. A lady who had remained beside me since we had first taken to the river, and who, like all the others, had remained silent till then, now asked me:

"Father, do you not think this is the end of the world?"

"I do not think so," was my reply, "but if other countries are burned as ours seems to have been, the end of the world, at least for us, must be at hand."

After this both relapsed into silence.

There is an end to all things here below, even misfortune. The longed-for moment of our return to land was at length arriving, and already sprinkling of our heads was becoming unnecessary. I drew near the bank, seated myself on a log, being in this manner only partly immersed in the water. Here I was seized with a violent chill. A young man perceiving it threw a blanket over me which at once afforded me relief, and soon after I was able to leave this compulsory bath in which I had been plunged for about five hours and a half.

🔥🔥🔥🔥🔥

CAME OUT OF THE RIVER ABOUT HALF PAST THREE IN THE morning, and from that time I was in a very different condition, both morally and physically, to that in which I had previously been. Today, in recalling the past, I can see that the moment most fraught with danger was precisely that in which danger seemed at an end. The atmosphere, previously hot as the breath of a furnace, was gradually becoming colder and colder, and, after having been so long in the river, I was of course exceedingly susceptible to its chilly influence. My clothes were thoroughly saturated. There was no want of fire, and I easily dried my outer garments, but the inner ones were wet, and their searching dampness penetrated to my inmost frame, affecting my very lungs. Though close to a large fire, arising from heaps of burning fragments, I was still convulsively shivering, feeling at the same time a complete prostration of body and spirit. My chest was oppressed to suffocation, my throat swollen, and, in addition to an almost total inability to move, I could scarcely use my voice—utter even a word.

WHi (X3) 51318

A June, 1867, view of the mill dam and sash factory at Peshtigo, before the tragic fire.

WHi (X3) 51321

The ruins of one of Peshtigo's factories bespeak the totality of the fire.

Almost lifeless, I stretched myself out full length on the sand. The latter was still hot, and the warmth in some degree restored me. Removing shoes and socks I placed my feet in immediate contact with the heated ground, and felt additionally relieved.

I was lying beside the ruins of the large factory, the beams of which were still burning. Around me were piles of iron hoops belonging to the tubs and buckets lately destroyed.[6] With the intention of employing these latter to dry my socks and shoes, now the only possessions left me, I touched them but found that they were still intolerably hot. Yet, strange to say, numbers of men were lying— some face downward—across these iron circles. Whether they were dead, or, rendered almost insensible from the effects of damp and cold, were seeking the warmth that the sand afforded me, I cannot say; I was suffering too intensely myself to attend to them.

My eyes were now beginning to cause me the most acute pain, and this proved the case, to a greater or less extent, with all those who had not covered theirs during the long storm of fire through which we had passed. Notwithstanding I had kept head and face streaming with water, the heat had nevertheless injured my eyes greatly, though at the moment I was almost unconscious of the circumstance. The intense pain they now caused, joined to a feeling of utter exhaustion, kept me for a length of time extended on the earth. When able, I dried my wet garments, one after the other, at the blazing ruins, and those near me did the same. As each individual thought of himself, without minding his neighbor, the task was easy even to the most scrupulous and delicate. Putting on dry clothes afforded immediate relief to the pain and oppression of my chest, enabling me to breathe with more ease. Finally day dawned on a scene with whose horror and ruin none were as yet fully acquainted. I received a friendly summons to proceed to another spot where the greater number of those who had escaped were assembled, but the inflammation of my eyes had rapidly augmented, and I was now perfectly blind. Someone led me, however, to the place of refuge. It was a little valley near the river's edge, completely sheltered by sand hills, and proved to be the very place where I had intended taking refuge the evening previous, though prevented reaching it by the violence of the hurricane. Some had succeeded in attaining it, and had suffered comparatively far less than we had done. The tempest of fire had passed, as it were, above this spot, leaving untouched the shrubs and plants growing within it.

Behold us then, all assembled in this valley like the survivors after a battle—some safe and well, others more or less wounded; some were very much so, especially a poor old woman who, fearing to enter the river completely, had lain crouched on the bank, partly in the water, partly out of it, and, consequently, exposed to the flames. She was now stretched on the grass, fearfully burned, and suffering intense agony, to judge from her heart-rending moans and cries. As she was dying, and had asked for me, I was brought to her, though I fear I proved but a poor consoler. I could not unclose my inflamed eyes, could scarcely speak, and felt so exhausted and depressed myself, that it was difficult to impart courage to others. The poor sufferer died shortly after.

Those among us who had sufficient strength for the task dispersed in different directions to seek information concerning the friends whom they had not yet seen, and returned with appalling tidings relating to the general ruin and the number of deaths by fire. One of these told me that they had crossed to the other side of the river, and found all the houses as well as the church in ashes, while numbers of corpses were lying by the wayside, so much disfigured by fire as to be beyond recognition.

"Well," I replied, "since it is thus, we will all proceed to Marinette, where there is a fine church, new presbytery, and school house, capable of lodging a great number."

About eight o'clock, a large tent, brought on by the Company, was erected for the purpose of sheltering the women, children, and the sick. As soon as it was prepared someone came and urged me to profit of it. I complied, and stretched myself in a corner, taking up as little place as possible, so as to leave room for others. But the man employed by the Company to superintend the erection of the tent had evidently escaped all injury to his eyes during the night, for he perceived me at once. He was one of those coarse and brutal natures that seem inaccessible to every kindly feeling though he manifested a remarkable interest in the welfare of the ladies, and would allow none but them under his tent. As soon as his glance fell on me he ordered me out, accompanying the rude command with a perfect torrent of insulting words and blasphemies. Without reply I turned over, passing beneath the canvass, and quickly found myself outside. One of the ladies present raised her voice in my defense, and vainly sought to give him a lesson in politeness. I never heard the name of this man, and rejoice that it is unknown to me.

Ten o'clock arrived. After the sufferings of the night previous, many longed for a cup of hot tea or coffee, but such a luxury was entirely out of our reach, amid the desolation and ruin surrounding us. Some of the young men, after a close search, found and brought back a few cabbages from a neighboring field. The outer leaves, which were thoroughly scorched, were removed, and the inner part cut into thin slices and distributed among those capable of eating them. A morsel of cold raw cabbage was not likely to prove of much use in our then state of exhaustion, but we had nothing better at hand.

At length the people of Marinette were informed of our condition, and, about one o'clock, several vehicles laden with bread, coffee, and tea arrived. These vehicles were commissioned at the same time to bring back as many of our number as they could contain. Anxious to obtain news from Marinette, I enquired of one of the men sent to our assistance if Marinette had also suffered from the fiery scourge.

"Thank God, Father, no one perished, though all were dreadfully alarmed. We have had many houses, however, burned. All the mills

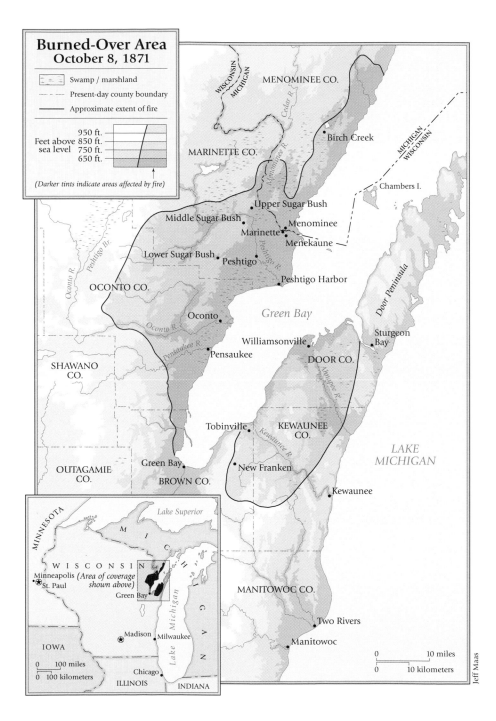

Burned-Over Area
October 8, 1871

Swamp / marshland
Present-day county boundary
Approximate extent of fire

950 ft.
Feet above 850 ft.
sea level 750 ft.
650 ft.

(Darker tints indicate areas affected by fire)

WISCONSIN
MICHIGAN

MENOMINEE CO.

Cedar R.

Birch Creek

MARINETTE CO.

Menominee R.

MICHIGAN
WISCONSIN

Chambers I.

Upper Sugar Bush

Middle Sugar Bush

Menominee

Marinette

Menekaune

Peshtigo Br.

Lower Sugar Bush

Peshtigo

Peshtigo R.

Peshtigo Harbor

Oconto R.

OCONTO CO.

Door Peninsula

Oconto

Green Bay

Oconto R.

Pensaukee R.

Williamsonville

Sturgeon Bay

Pensaukee

DOOR CO.

SHAWANO CO.

Ahnapee R.

Tobinville

KEWAUNEE CO.

Kewaunee R.

LAKE MICHIGAN

OUTAGAMIE CO.

Green Bay

New Franken

BROWN CO.

Kewaunee

MINNESOTA

Lake Superior

M I C H I G A N

W I S C O N S I N

Minneapolis
St. Paul

(Area of coverage shown above)

Green Bay

IOWA

Madison

Milwaukee

Lake Michigan

MANITOWOC CO.

Two Rivers

0   100 miles
0   100 kilometers

Chicago

Manitowoc

ILLINOIS

INDIANA

0   10 miles
0   10 kilometers

Jeff Maas

and houses from our church down to the Bay have gone."

"And the church?"

"It is burned."

"The handsome presbytery?"

"Burned."

"The new schoolhouse?"

"Burned also."

Ah! And I had promised the poor unfortunates of Peshtigo to bring them to Marinette and shelter them in those very buildings. Thus I found myself bereft in the same hour of my two churches, two presbyteries, and schoolhouse, as well as of all private property belonging to them or to myself.

❧❧❧❧❧

BETWEEN ONE AND TWO O'CLOCK I LEFT IN ONE OF THE wagons for Marinette, and after arriving there, sojourned for some time at the residence of one of my parishioners, Mr. F. Garon, receiving under his hospitable roof all the care my condition required.

The two banks of the river respectively named Marinette and Menominee and which, united, formed another parish, were strangely changed in appearance. These two sister towns, one situated on the south and the other on the north side of the river, were no longer recognizable. Life and activity had entirely given place to silence and a species of woeful stupefaction. A few men only were to be seen going backwards and forwards, looking after their property, or asking details concerning the conflagration at Peshtigo from those who had just arrived from that ill-fated spot. No women were to be seen in the streets nor even in the houses, the latter having been abandoned. The children, too, with their joyous outcries and noisy mirth had disappeared from the scene. These shores, a short while since so animated, now resembled a desert, and it was a movement of overwhelming and uncontrollable terror that had created, as it were, this solitude, a terror which dated from the preceding night when the tempest of fire came surging on from Peshtigo, consuming all that part of Marinette that lay in its path. Intelligence of the fate that had overtaken Peshtigo farther increased this general feeling of alarm till it culminated in a perfect panic. Dreading a similar catastrophe to that of Peshtigo, many families hastened towards the Bay, embarking on the steamers, *Union, Dunlap,* and *St. Joseph,* which had been kept near the shore so as to afford a refuge to the terrified inhabitants. The consternation was indescribable, and one unfortunate man on arriving panting and breathless at the boat fell dead from fear or exhaustion. These boats afforded anything but a safe place of refuge, for if the conflagration had broken out as suddenly and raged as fiercely as it had done at Peshtigo, nothing could have preserved them from the flames, and the only alternative left to those on board would have been death by fire or water. Fear, however, is generally an untrustworthy counsellor, and the expedients it suggests remarkably ill chosen. The inhabitants of Marinette and Menominee passed the night of October eighth dispersed in the different boats, and it is unnecessary to add that few slept during those hours of strange anxiety. Terror effectually banished slumber, producing the result fear generally does on the Christian soul, turning it instinctively to prayer, even as the terror-stricken child casts itself into the arms of the mother it has summoned to its help. What are we, poor mortals, exposed to the wild fury of the unchained elements, but helpless children? The Catholics present with one accord cast themselves on their knees and prayed aloud, imploring the Ruler of the elements to stay His vengeful arm and spare His people. They prayed without shyness or human respect. Doubtless, there were present those who had perhaps never learned to pray, or who had forgotten how to accomplish that all important duty, and these latter might in other circumstances have felt annoyed at such public manifestations of devotion, but in this hour of common peril, all hearts involuntarily turned towards heaven as their only resource. There were no tokens of incredulity, impiety, or bigotry evinced by any. The Protestants who were present, being unacquainted with the Catholic formula of prayer, could not unite their supplications with those of the latter, but they encouraged them to continue their devotions, and when they paused, solicited them to recommence. Danger is a successful teacher, its influence immediate and irresistible. No reasoning succeeds so quickly in making men comprehend the greatness of God and their own helplessness. Naught else detaches souls so completely from earth and raises them towards Him on whom we all depend.

The preceding details, furnished by individuals coming and going from the boats, were full of interest to me. During this time I remained with my kind host, Mr. Garon, being too ill even to leave the house. The kind attentions of which I was the object soon restored me in some degree to health. Tuesday evening, I was able to visit several persons who had been injured more or less grievously by fire, and to prepare the dying for their last end, as far as lay in my power, in the total absence of everything necessary on the sad occasion. Feeling strong enough, I resolved to return to Peshtigo on Tuesday night, and commenced my preparations. The clothes I wore had been greatly injured by my long sojourn in the water, and I would have willingly replaced them, but found this impossible. The storekeepers, fearing a similar misfortune to that which had overtaken the merchants of Peshtigo, had packed up the greater part of their merchandise and buried it. I could get nothing save a suit of coarse yellow material such as workmen wear whilst engaged in sawmills. In the absence of something better it had to answer, and about ten o'clock at night I went on board a steamboat about leaving for Green Bay, calling previously, however, at Peshtigo. The night was very stormy, and it was only about daybreak that we ventured to land, the water being very rough when we reached Peshtigo landing, which was about nine or ten in the morning. I remained there only a few hours, during which time I visited the sick beds of several victims of the conflagration.

About one o'clock in the afternoon a car was leaving for Peshtigo, conveying thither men who went daily there for the purpose of seeking out and burying the dead. I took my place with them. The locomotives belonging to the Company, having been burned, were now replaced by horses, and we progressed thus till we came up with the track of the fire. We walked the rest of the way, a distance of half a league, and this gave me ample opportunity for examining thoroughly the devastation and ruin wrought, both by fire and by wind. Alas, much as I had heard on the sad subject, I was still unprepared for the melancholy spectacle that met my gaze.

It is a painful thing to have to speak of scenes which we feel convinced no pen could fully describe nor words do justice to. It was on the eleventh of October, Wednesday afternoon, that I revisited for the first time the site of what had once been the town of Peshtigo. Of the houses, trees, fences that I had looked on three days ago nothing whatever remained, save a few blackened posts still standing, as if to attest the impetuous fury of the fiery element that had thus destroyed

WHi (X3) 51320

After the fire, ashes and debris were all that remained in Peshtigo.

all before it. Wherever the foot chanced to fall it rested on ashes. The iron tracks of the railroad had been twisted and curved into all sorts of shapes, whilst the wood which had supported them no longer existed. The trunks of mighty trees had been reduced to mere cinders, the blackened hearts alone remaining. All around these trunks, I perceived a number of holes running downwards deep in the earth. They were the sockets where the roots had lately been. I plunged my cane into one of them, thinking what must the violence of that fire have been, which ravaged not only the surface of the earth, but penetrated so deeply into its bosom. Then I turned my wondering gaze in the direction where the town had lately stood, but nothing remained to point out its site except the boilers of the two locomotives, the iron of the wagon wheels, and the brick and stonework of the factory. All the rest was a desert the desolation of which was sufficient to draw tears from the eyes of the spectator—a desert recalling a field of battle after a sanguinary conflict. Charred carcasses of horses, cows, oxen, and other animals lay scattered here and there.[7] The bodies of the human victims—men, women, and children—had been already collected and decently interred—their number being easily ascertained by counting rows of freshly-made graves. To find the streets was a difficult task, and it was not without considerable trouble that I succeeded at length in ascertaining the site where my house had lately stood. My next care was to look for the spot where I had buried my trunks and other valuables. This I discovered by means of the shovel which I had employed in digging the trench and which I had thrown to a short distance, my task completed. There it still lay, half of the handle burned off, the rest in good order, and I employed it once again to disinter my effects. On moving the sand, a disagreeable odor, somewhat resembling that of brimstone, exhaled from it. My linen appeared at the first glance to be in a state of perfect preservation, having kept even its whiteness, with the exception of the pleats, which were somewhat discolored; but on touching it, it fell to pieces as if the substance had been consumed by some slow, peculiar process, or traversed by electricity. Whilst touching on this subject we may add that many felt a shock of earthquake at the moment that everything on the surface of the earth

was trembling before the violence of the hurricane. Here again was a total loss. A few calcined bricks, melted crystal, with crosses and crucifixes more or less destroyed, alone pointed out where my house had once been, while the charred remains of my poor dog indicated the site of my bedroom. I followed then the road leading from my house to the river, and which was the one I had taken on the night of the catastrophe. There, the carcasses of animals were more numerous than elsewhere, especially in the neighborhood of the bridge. I saw the remains of my poor horse in the spot where I had last met him, but so disfigured by the fiery death through which he had passed that I had some difficulty in recognizing him.

Like this deer, many animals perished in the fire, including Reverend Pernin's horse and dog.

WHi (X3) 51324

45

Those who have a horse, and appreciate the valuable services he renders them, will not feel surprised at my speaking twice of mine. There exists between the horse and his master a species of friendship akin to that which unites two friends, and which in the man frequently survives the death of his four-footed companion.

Whilst wandering among the ruins I met several persons, with some of whom I entered into conversation. One was a bereaved father seeking his missing children of whom he had as yet learned nothing. "If, at least," he said to me, with a look of indescribable anguish, "I could find their bones, but the wind has swept away whatever the fire spared." Children were seeking for their parents, brothers for their brothers, husbands for their wives, but I saw no women amid this scene of horror which it would have been almost impossible for them to contemplate. The men I met, those sorrowful seekers for the dead, had all suffered more or less in the battle against wind and fire. Some had had a hand burned, others an arm or side; all were clothed in blackened, ragged garments, appearing, each one from his look of woeful sadness and miserable condition, like a ruin among ruins. They pointed out to me the places where they had found such and such individuals: there a mother lay prone on her face, pressing to her bosom the child she had vainly striven to save from the devouring element; here a whole family, father, mother, and children, lying together, blackened and mutilated by the fire fiend. Among the ruins of the boarding house belonging to the Company, more than seventy bodies were found, disfigured to such a fearful extent that it was impossible to tell either their age or sex. Farther on twenty more had been drawn from a well. One of the workmen engaged in the construction of the church was found, knife in hand, with his throat cut, two of his children lying beside him in a similar condition; while his wife lay a little farther off, having evidently been burned to death. The name of this man was Towsley,[8] and during the whole summer he had worked at the church of Peshtigo. Doubtless seeing his wife fall near him, and becoming convinced of the utter impossibility of escaping a fiery death, his mind became troubled, and he put an end to his own existence and that of his children. There were several other similar cases of suicide arising from the same sad causes.

These heartrending accounts, combined with the fearful desolation that met my gaze wherever it turned, froze my veins with horror!

Painting by Mel Kishner depicting the plight of the victims trapped in the Sugar Bush, far from the Peshtigo River.

🔥🔥🔥🔥🔥

ALAS! THAT I SHOULD HAVE TO RECORD AN INCIDENT such as should never have happened in the midst of that woeful scene! Whilst struggling with the painful impressions produced in my mind by the spectacle on which I looked, my attention was attracted to another quarter by the sound of voices, raised in loud excitement. The cause of the tumult was this: In the midst of the universal consternation pervading all minds, a man was found degraded enough to insult not only the general sorrow and mourning but also death itself. Enslaved by the wretched vice of avarice, he had just been taken in the act of despoiling the bodies of the dead of whatever objects the fire had spared. A jury was formed, his punishment put to the vote, and he was unanimously condemned to be hanged on the spot. But where was a rope to be found? The fire had spared nothing. Somebody proposed substituting for the former an iron chain which had been employed for drawing logs, and one was accordingly brought and placed around the criminal's neck. Execution was difficult under the circumstances; and whilst the preparations dragged slowly on, the miserable man loudly implored mercy. The pity inspired by the mournful surroundings softened at length the hearts of the judges, and, after having made him crave pardon on his knees for the sacrilegious thefts of which he had been guilty, they allowed him to go free. It may have been that they merely intended frightening him.

Weary of noise and tumult, and longing for solitude, I left my previous companions, and followed for a considerable distance that road to Oconto on which I had seen so many vehicles entering, turning their backs on the river to which I was hastening with the tabernacle. I had not gone far before I saw much more than I would have desired to see. All in this line had perished, and perished in masses, for the vehicles were crowded with unfortunates who, flying from death, had met it all the sooner and in its most horrible form. In those places where the flames had enfolded their victims in their fiery clasp, nothing now was to be seen but calcined bones, charred mortal remains, and the iron circles of the wheels. It was with some difficulty that the human relics could be distinguished from those of the horses. The workmen of the Company were employed in collecting these sad memorials and burying them by the wayside, there to remain till such time as the friends of the dead might wish to reclaim and inter them in a more suitable manner.

I left them at their mournful task, and returned to the site where our church had so lately stood. There also all was in ashes, nothing remaining save the church bell. The latter had been thrown a distance of fifty feet; one half was now lying there intact, while the other part had melted and spread over the sand in silvery leaves. The voice of this bell had been the last sound heard in the midst of the hurricane. Its lugubrious note yet seems at times to strike on my ear, reminding me of the horrors of which it was a forerunner.

The graveyard lay close to the church, and I entered and waited there; for I expected momentarily the arrival of a funeral. It was that of a young man who had died the evening previous, in consequence of the terrible burns he had received. Never was burial service more poverty-stricken nor priest more utterly destitute of all things necessary for the performance of the sad ceremony. Nor church, nor house, nor surplice, stole nor breviary: nothing save prayer and a heartfelt benediction. I had felt this destitution still more keenly on two or three previous occasions when asked by the dying for the sacrament of Extreme Unction, which it was out of my power, alas, to administer to them. I left the graveyard with a heavy heart, and turned my steps in the direction of the river, which I had to cross in order to seek for my tabernacle with whose ultimate fate I was unacquainted. A bright ray of consolation awaited me and seldom was consolation more needed.

I crossed the river on the half-charred beams of the bridge which had been joined together so as to offer a means of passage, though a very perilous one, to those who chose to trust themselves to it. I had barely reached the other side when one of my parishioners hastened to meet me, joyfully exclaiming: "Father, do you know what has happened to your tabernacle?"

"No, what is it?"

"Come quickly then, and see. Oh! Father, it is a great miracle!"

I hurried with him to that part of the river into which I had pushed as far as possible my wagon containing the tabernacle. This wagon had been blown over on its side by the storm; whilst the tabernacle itself had been caught up by the wind and cast on one of the logs floating on the water. Everything in the immediate vicinity of this spot had been blackened or charred by the flames; logs, trunks, boxes, nothing had escaped, yet, strange to say, there rose the tabernacle, intact in its showy whiteness, presenting a wonderful contrast to the grimy blackness of the surrounding objects. I left it in the spot where it had thus been thrown by the tempest for two days, so as to give all an opportunity of seeing it. Numbers came, though of course in that time of horror and desolation there were many too deeply engrossed with their own private griefs to pay attention to aught else. The Catholics generally regarded the fact as a miracle, and it was spoken of near and far, attracting great attention.

Alas! Nothing is more evanescent than the salutary impressions produced on the mind of man by divine blessings or punishments. Time and the preoccupations of life efface even the very remembrance of them. How few there are among the rare survivors of the fire that swept Peshtigo from the face of the earth who still see the power of God in the calamity that then overwhelmed them as well as in the preservation of the tabernacle, events which at the time of their occurrence made so deep an impression on their minds.

When the duties which had detained me three days amid these mournful scenes were completed, I took the tabernacle from the place which it had occupied of late and sent it on to Marinette where I intended soon saying mass. When the right time arrived, I forcibly opened the tiny door. There—circumstance as wonderful as the preservation of the tabernacle in the midst of the conflagration—I found the consecrated Host intact in the monstrance while the violent concussions the ciborium must have undergone had not caused it even to open. Water had not penetrated within, and the flames had respected the interior as well as exterior, even to the silky tissue lining the sides. All was in a state of perfect preservation!

These sacred objects, though possessing in reality but little intrinsic value, are nevertheless priceless in my eyes. I prize them as most precious relics, and never look at or touch them without feeling penetrated with sentiments of love and veneration such as no other holy vessels, however rich and beautiful, could awake within me. In the little chapel at Marinette, which replaces the church burned there more than two years ago, the same tabernacle is on the altar and contains the same monstrance and ciborium which were so wonderfully preserved from the flames, and, daily, during the holy sacrifice, I use them with a species of religious triumph as trophies of God's exceeding mercy snatched so marvellously from destruction.

I must beg my readers to return with me for a little while to the banks of Peshtigo River—but not to linger there long. Before removing the tabernacle I was busily occupied three days and two nights, now in seeking for the dead, then in taking up from the water various objects which I had thrown by armfuls, at the moment of leaving my house, into the wagon and which had been overturned with it into the river. The most precious of all these was the chalice, which I was fortunate enough to find, together with the paten. My search was greatly facilitated by the opening of the dam and letting out of the waters which were here fifteen or twenty feet in depth. This step was necessary for the finding of the corpses of those persons who, either seized by cramps, or drawn in by the current, had been drowned during the night of the hurricane.

For the space of these three days our only habitation was the tent, the shelter of which had been so arbitrarily refused me the preceding Monday. It covered us during our meals, which we took standing and as best we could, and during the night protected the slumbers of those who could sleep, a thing I found impossible. Our beds were made on a most economical plan—the river sand formed our substitute for mattresses, and a single blanket constituted our covering.

During this period I first learned the fate of the city of Chicago. A physician, come from Fond du Lac to attend to the sick and burned, brought a newspaper with him and in it we read of the terrible ravages wrought by fire, on the same night, and, strange to say, about the same hour, not only at Peshtigo but in many other places and above all at Chicago. This great conflagration at Chicago proclaimed to the world by the myriad voices of journal and telegraph, created far and wide an immense outburst of compassion in favor of the fortunate city, diverting entirely the general attention from the far more appalling calamities of which we had been the hapless victims.

51

❧❧❧❧❧

ON THE AFTERNOON OF FRIDAY, THE THIRTEENTH, I HAD about finished my labors on the desolate banks of Peshtigo River. The corpses found had all been decently interred, and the sick and maimed carried to different places of safety. Exhausted with fatigue and privation, I felt I could not bear up much longer, and accordingly took place in a wagon that had brought us supplies, and was now returning to Oconto in which latter town I had friends who were awaiting my arrival with friendly impatience. I enjoyed two days of the rest at the residence of Father Vermore [A. Vermere], the excellent parish priest of the French church. Monday following I left for Green Bay to visit his Lordship, Bishop Joseph Melcher, dead, alas, even now while I write these lines.

As often happens in such cases, the most contradictory rumors had been circulated with regard to myself. Some declared that I had been burned in the church whither I had gone to pray a moment previous to the outburst of the storm, others asserted that I had met a fiery death in my own abode, whilst many were equally positive that I had perished in the river.

On seeing me the Bishop, who had naturally been rendered anxious by these contradictory reports, eagerly exclaimed: "Oh! at last! I have been so troubled about you! Why did you not write?" "My Lord, I could not," was my reply, "I had neither pen, ink, nor paper, nothing but river water."

He generously offered me every thing I required, either from his library or wardrobe, but I declined the kind offer, as there were still a number of my parishioners on the river Menominee and it was for them to help, not him. He then wished to appoint me to another parish, declaring that I merited repose after all I had endured, and that a farther sojourn among my people, poor and decimated in number, would be only a continuation of suffering and hard toil. Remembering, however, that my parishioners would thus be left without a priest at a time when the ministrations of one would be doubly necessary to them, recalling, also, how much better it was that their poverty and privations should be shared by one who knew and loved them, I solicited and obtained permission to remain among my flock. Soon, however, the sufferings I had endured began to tell on my constitution; and to such an extent that, having been invited by the

Rev. Mr. [P.] Crud, parish priest of Green Bay, to preach on All Saints, he was told by Bishop Melcher he must not count on me as my brain was seriously injured by the fiery ordeal through which I had passed. I cannot well say whether this was really the case. I know that I was terribly feeble, and hoping that a few months' repose might restore my health, I resolved to travel, determined to make the trip conducive at the same time to the welfare of my impoverished parishes. My first intention was to visit Louisiana returning by the East, but I was destined soon to learn that my strength was unequal to the task. Arrived at St. Louis, I was attacked by a fever that kept me confined to the bed each day for three or four hours, and which made sad inroads on the small stock of health left me. Accordingly I went no farther. The kind people of St. Louis showed me a great deal of sympathy, and I made friends among them whom I can never forget, and whom meeting with once more would be a source of great pleasure. I will not mention their names here, but they are written on my heart in ineffaceable characters. I can do nothing myself to prove my gratitude, but I will whisper their names to our most powerful and most clement Lady of Lourdes, in her church of Marinette, and she will atone for my incapacity.

Having mentioned the claims of the inhabitants of St. Louis on my gratitude, it would be unjust on my part to pass in silence over those of my own parishioners and friends in Wisconsin, who spontaneously offered me help in the first moments of distress. Ah, they are not forgotten! Very pleasant is it to recall these warm expressions of sympathy, springing directly from the heart. Amongst many similar traits, well do I remember the words of a friend in Oconto who, wishing me to accept decent garments to replace those which I had brought back from the conflagration exclaimed on my persistent refusal, "I insist, for well I know that, if I happened to be in your place, you would equally desire to render me a similar service."

🔥🔥🔥🔥🔥

IT MAY BE AS WELL TO RECORD HERE SOME OF THE extraordinary phenomena and peculiar characteristics of the strange fire that wrought so much desolation, though I was not personally a witness to them all. I was too near the inner portion of the circle to be able to see much of what was passing on the outside. It is not he who is in the middle of the combat that has the best view of the battle and its details, but rather the man who contemplates it from some elevated point overlooking the plain.

Whole forests of huge maples, deeply and strongly rooted in the soil, were torn up, twisted and broken, as if they had been willow wands. A tree standing upright here or there was an exception to an almost general rule. There lay those children of the forest, heaped up one over the other in all imaginable positions, their branches reduced to cinders, and their trunks calcined and blackened. Many asseverated that they had seen large wooden houses torn from their foundations and caught up like straws by two opposing currents of air which raised them till they came in contact with the stream of fire. They then burst into flames, and, exposed thus to the fury of two fierce elements, wind and fire, were torn to pieces and reduced to ashes almost simultaneously.

Still, the swiftness with which this hurricane, seemingly composed of wind and fire together, advanced, was in no degree proportioned to its terrible force. By computing the length of time that elapsed between the rising of the tempest in the southwest, and its subsiding in the northeast, it will be easily seen that the rate of motion did not exceed two leagues an hour. The hurricane moved in a circle, advancing slowly, as if to give time to prepare for its coming.

Many circumstances tended to prove that the intensity of the heat produced by the fire was in some places extreme, nay unheard of. I have already mentioned that the flames pursued the roots of the trees into the very depths of the earth, consuming them to the last inch. I plunged my cane down into these cavities, and convinced myself that nothing had stayed the course of combustion save the utter want of anything to feed on. Hogsheads of nails were found entirely melted though lying outside the direct path of the flames. Immense numbers of fish of all sizes died, and the morning after the storm the river was covered with them. It would be impossible to decide what was the cause of their death. It may have been owing to the intensity of the heat, the want of air necessary to respiration—the air being violently sucked in by the current tending upwards to that fierce focus of flame or they may have been killed by some poisonous gas.

It is more than probable that for a moment the air was impregnated with an inflammable gas most destructive to human life.

I have already mentioned the tiny globules of fire flying about my house at the moment I quitted it. Whilst on my way to the river, I met now and then gusts of an air utterly unfit for respiration, and was obliged on these occasions to throw myself on the ground to regain my breath, unless already prostrated involuntarily by the violence of the wind. Whilst standing in the river I had noticed, as I have already related, on casting my eye upwards, a sea of flame, as it were, the immense waves of which were in a state of violent commotion, rolling tumultuously one over the other, and all at a prodigious height in the sky, and, consequently, far from any combustible material. How can this phenomenon be explained without admitting the supposition that immense quantities of gas were accumulated in the air?[9]

Strange to say there were many corpses found, bearing about them no traces of scars or burns, and yet in the pockets of their habiliments, equally uninjured, watches, cents, and other articles in metal were discovered completely melted. How was it also that many escaped with their lives here and there on the cleared land as well as in the woods? The problem is a difficult one to solve. The tempest did not rage in all parts with equal fury, but escape from its power was a mere affair of chance. None could boast of having displayed more presence of mind than others. Generally speaking, those who happened to be in low lying lands, especially close to excavations or even freshly ploughed earth with which they could cover themselves, as the Indians do, succeeded in saving their lives. Most frequently the torrent of fire passed at a certain height from the earth, touching only the most elevated portions. Thus no one could meet it standing erect without paying the penalty of almost instantaneous death.

When the hurricane burst upon us, many, surprised and terrified, ran out to see what was the matter. A number of these persons assert that they then witnessed a phenomenon which may be classed with the marvelous. They saw a large black object, resembling a balloon, which object revolved in the air with great rapidity, advancing above the summits of the trees towards a house which it seemed to single out for destruction. Barely had it touched the latter when the balloon burst with a loud report, like that of a bombshell, and, at the same moment, rivulets of fire streamed out in all directions. With the rapidity of thought, the house thus chosen was enveloped in flames within and without, so that the persons inside had no time for escape.

WHi (X3) 28471

Ten years after the fire, Peshtigo had risen from the ashes, as this bird's-eye view from 1881 indicates.

It is somewhat difficult to calculate the extent of territory overrun by the fiery scourge, on account of the irregularity of the course followed by the latter. Still, without exaggeration, the surface thus ravaged, extending from the southwest to the northeast of Peshtigo, may be set down as not far from fifteen to twenty leagues in length by five or six in width. The number of deaths in Peshtigo, including the farmers dwelling in the environs, was not less than one thousand—that is to say, about half of the population. More than eight hundred known individuals had disappeared; but there were crowds of strangers, many of whom had arrived that very morning, whose names had not been registered, and whose number will ever remain unknown.

Among those who escaped from the awful scourge, many have since died, owing to the hardships then endured, whilst others are dropping off day by day. A physician belonging to Green Bay has predicted that before ten years all the unfortunate survivors of that terrible catastrophe will have paid the debt of nature, victims of the irreparable injury inflicted on their constitutions by smoke, air, water, and fire.[10] If the prediction continues to be as faithfully realized in the future as it has been in the past, my turn will also come.

May the construction of the Church of Our Lady of Lourdes, at Marinette, be then completed, so that some grateful hearts may pray there for the repose of my soul.

❧EPILOGUE❧

From Peshtigo the fire roared toward Marinette, destroying Father Pernin's other church and its newly built presbyter but leaving the village mainly intact. Then the fire split into two forks, the one on the right going on to consume the village of Menekaunee, the one on the left jumping the Menominee River to ravage the Birch Creek settlement in Michigan, killing eight men, two women, and twelve children.

Some sources have estimated the number of dead as 1,200. The *Encyclopedia Britannica* gives a total of 1,152, evidently using the figure arrived at by Stewart Holbrook in his *Burning an Empire*. However, the true total will never be known, since whole farmsteads were erased, leaving no trace, and no one knows how many itinerant workers died in Peshtigo's company boardinghouse or in its two churches, to which many fled in panic, or in isolated logging camps deep in the surrounding woods. People simply became piles of ashes or calcinated bones, identifiable only if a buckle, a ring, a shawl pin, or some other familiar object survived the incredible heat. A painstaking, three-month investigation by Colonel J. H. Leavenworth, as printed in the *Assembly Journal* for 1873, lists the names of only 383 identified dead: 77 in Peshtigo, 12 in Lincoln, 50 in Brussels, 3 in Nasawanpee, and 2 in Birch Creek, Michigan. The heaviest losses were in the Sugar Bushes, where no convenient river furnished a refuge from the flames. Here a total of 241 identified bodies were found, of whom 123 were children. How many died subsequently or were maimed for life is not known. At any rate, according to Leavenworth's report, a year after the event many survivors remained partially or permanently demented as a result of their ordeal.

News of the disaster did not immediately reach the outside world. Isaac Stephenson, the Marinette lumber baron, on learning of Peshtigo's fate, had an emissary sent to Green Bay—the nearest place where the telegraph lines had not been burned out—to transmit a message to Governor Lucius Fairchild. The message did not reach Madison until the morning of the tenth. Fairchild and all state officials were in Chicago, whence they had gone with carloads of supplies to aid the stricken city. A capitol clerk took the telegram to the governor's wife, Frances Fairchild, who immediately swung into action. For a day this remarkable woman, then younger than twenty-

57

four, was to all intents and purposes the governor of Wisconsin. As her daughter, Mary Fairchild Morris, recalled in a letter to Joseph Schafer in May, 1927, commandeered a boxcar loaded with supplies destined for Chicago, ordered railroad officials to give it priority over all other traffic, and then, discovering that the car contained food and clothing but no defenses against the October cold, rallied Madison women to supply blankets to stuff into the already loaded car. After the car was dispatched, Mrs. Fairchild issued a public appeal for

Frances Fairchild
WHi (X3) 12521

contributions of money, clothing, bedding, and supplies, with the result that a second boxcar left Madison that night.

Immediately on receiving the news of the Peshtigo disaster, relief committees were organized in Green Bay, Oconto, and Marinette; emergency hospitals were set up for the injured, and lodgings were found for the homeless survivors. Eventually the Green Bay Relief Committee was augmented by a second in Milwaukee, and hardly a community in the state failed to establish some kind of relief organization. Following Governor Fairchild's broadcast appeal for aid, contributions began to pour in from all over the state, the nation, and several foreign countries. In all, $166,789 was collected in cash donations, while the U.S. government contributed from army supplies 4,000 woolen blankets, 1,500 pairs of trousers and overcoats, 100 wagons with sets of harness, and 200,000 rations of hard bread, beans, bacon, dried beef, pork, sugar, rice, coffee, and the like.

Slowly the devastated area began to recover. Schoolhouses and bridges were rebuilt, roads were repaired. Despite his substantial losses, William G. Ogden ordered that his woodenware company be rebuilt; others followed suit, and Peshtigo struggled back to life. In January, 1873, Governor Cadwallader C. Washburn, who had succeeded Lucius Fairchild, reported in the *Assembly Journal*: "In the month of July I visited the burnt district on the peninsula, as well as on the west side of Green Bay. I found the devastation produced by the fire fiend such as is impossible for the mind to comprehend without the aid of the eye. I was pleased to find that a majority of the survivors had returned to their clearings; many had raised fair crops, and were hopeful of the future."

Part of the process of reconstruction included the rebuilding of Father Pernin's church, Our Lady of Lourdes. It still stands today on Main Street in Marinette as a part of Central Catholic High School, its sanctuary serving as a chapel and the remainder of the building as a rehearsal hall.

❧ENDNOTES❧

1.   There were three of these farming communities: the Lower Sugar Bush, comprising settlements extending for about seven miles west of Peshtigo on the road leading to Oconto; the Middle Sugar Bush, made up of settlements along a road running to the southwest; and the Upper Sugar Bush, containing settlements along what was known as the Lake Noquebay Road. In all, they consisted of about 300 families. Frank Tilton, *Sketch of the Great Fires in Wisconsin at Peshtigo, the Sugar Bush, Menekaune, Williamsonville . . .* (Green Bay, 1871), 7.

2.   A league varies from about 2.4 miles to 4.6 statute miles, depending on the nation involved. Pernin was probably using the English league, which is about three miles, since Peshtigo is about seven miles from Marinette.

3.   The account is from the *Green Bay Advocate*, October 5, 1871.

4.   During early October the smoke was so dense on the Bay that during daylight hours navigation was done by compass, and foghorns were kept blowing continuously, the shores being invisible. *Green Bay Advocate*, October 5, 1871.

5.   The northern extension of the Chicago and North Western Railway from Fort Howard to Menominee and thence to Escanaba to connect with the iron mines in Upper Michigan was under construction. In clearing the right-of-way, many fires had been allowed to escape into the woods. Tilton, *Sketch of the Great Fires*, 10; letter dated July, 1927, from John J. Casson of Los Angeles, a mechanic at the Peshtigo woodenware mill and a survivor of the fire, in Archives-Manuscripts Division, State Historical Society of Wisconsin.

6.   John Casson says in the previously cited letter:, "All of the bodies were so badly charred we used iron barrel hoops under the necks and limbs to move them."

7.   All other accounts mention that in addition to the ruins noted by Father Pernin, a partially completed dwelling survived the disaster, one side of it had been burned to cinders, while the side facing the fire had not even been scorched. A photograph of the house, showing one of the charred beams, which was included in the final construction, appeared in the *Milwaukee Journal*, October 8, 1951. An appendix to the *Wisconsin Assembly Journal of Proceedings*, 1873, page 173, lists the following loss in property and livestock: 27 schoolhouses; 9 churches; 959 dwellings; 1,028 barns and stables; 116 horses; 157 working cattle;

266 cows and heifers; 201 sheep; and 306 hogs. The figures undoubtedly are incomplete, since many homesteads were so completely destroyed that no trace of any living thing could be found. The heaviest individual loser was William G. Ogden, the Chicago railroad magnate, who was reputed to have lost three million dollars in the Peshtigo and Chicago fires. Wells, *Fire at Peshtigo*, 142.

8. Although the implication here is that the bodies were found in Peshtigo, they were actually discovered in the Lower Sugar Bush. In the list of recognized bodies printed in the appendix to the *Assembly Journal, 1873*, the father is given as C. R. Tousley.

9. In his report to Governor C. C. Washburn, Captain A. J. Langworthy, chairman of the Green Bay Relief Committee, stoutly upheld the theory that inflammable gas, particularly marsh gas from peat swamps, that in the preceding weeks had often burned to a depth of three feet, played a major role in increasing the fire's intensity. He enclosed in his report a statement from Increase A. Lapham supporting the view that "carburetted hydrogen" produces great masses of combustible gas resembling balls of fire that would explode on contact with oxygen. Langworthy also included a letter from C. F. Chandler of the Columbia College School of Mines in New York flatly denying that combustible gases could be produced in the atmosphere. As a final clincher, Langworthy included depositions from Luther B. Noyes, Marinette judge and editor, and from a noted chemist on the faculty of the U.S. Naval Academy, both upholding the gas theory. In 1927 Joseph Schafer attempted a scientific explanation for the great fires of 1871, but it remained for Robert Wells, using research reports furnished by the U.S. Forest Service, to supply the most intelligible explanation for the origin and nature of the fire. Conceding that marsh gas may have played a minor role, Wells concludes that the convection column—a whirling chimney of superheated air generated by the fire— suddenly broke through the blanket of heavier, smoke-laden air into the colder air above, thus creating a huge updraft that led to the fire tornado, the whirlwinds, and the curious phenomena reported by survivors. See appendix to the *Assembly Journal, 1873*; Joseph Schafer, "Great Fires of Seventy-One," in the *Wisconsin Magazine of History*, 11:96–106 (September, 1927); and Wells, *Fire at Peshtigo*, 199–214.

10. Although many survivors subsequently died of their dreadful burns, and others were disabled for life, the unidentified physician's prediction fortunately did not hold true. When ceremonies were held

on the eightieth anniversary of the fire, in October, 1951, nineteen survivors were present to witness the unveiling of the first official state marker, erected in the refurbished Fire Cemetery. The oldest survivor was 96. As late as 1958, Fay S. Dooley, curator of Old Wade House and a former Peshtigo resident, was able to identify six survivors still living. *Milwaukee Journal*, October 8, 1951; *Peshtigo Times*, October 4, 1951; William F. Steuber, Jr., "The Problem at Peshtigo," in the *Wisconsin Magazine of History*, 43:13–15 (Autumn, 1958).

❧SELECTED BIBLIOGRAPHY❧

Pernin, P. (Pierre). *"The Finger of God Is There!, Or, Thrilling Episode of a Strange Event Related by an Eye-Witness, Published with the Approbation of His Lordship the Bishop of Montreal for the Church of Our Lady of Lourdes in Marinette, State of Wisconsin.* Montreal: J. Lovell, 1874; microfiche, Webster, New York: Photographic Sciences Corp., 1981.

Pernin, Peter. "The Great Peshtigo Fire: An Eyewitness Account," ed. William Converse Haygood, in the *Wisconsin Magazine of History*, 54:246–272 (Summer, 1971.)

Peshtigo Times. *Remembering the Peshtigo Fire.* Special edition of the *Peshtigo Times*, October 7, 1998. (The most recent of several special editions devoted to the history of the fire.)

Pyne, Stephen J. *Fire in America: A Cultural History of Wildland and Rural Fire.* Princeton, New Jersey: Princeton University Press, 1982.

Schafer, Joseph. "Editorial Comment: Great Fires of Seventy-One," in the *Wisconsin Magazine of History*, 11:96–106 (September, 1927.)

Sewell, Alfred L. *"The Great Calamity!" Scenes, Incidents and Lessons of the Great Chicago Fire of the 8th and 9th of October, 1871. Also Some Account of Other Great Conflagrations of Modern Times, and the Burning of Peshtigo, Wisconsin.* Chicago: A. L. Sewell, *1871.*

Steuber, William F., Jr. *The Landlooker.* Indianapolis: Bobbs-Merrill, 1974. (Historical novel.)

_____."The Problem at Peshtigo," in the *Wisconsin Magazine of History*, 42:13–15 (Autumn, 1958.)

Tilton, Frank. *Sketch of the Great Fires in Wisconsin at Peshtigo, the Sugar Bush, Menekaune, Williamsonville, and Generally on the Shores of Green Bay: With Thrilling and Truthful Incidents by Eye Witnesses.* Green Bay: Robinson & Kustermann, 1871.

Wells, Robert W. *Fire at Peshtigo.* Three editions: Englewood Cliffs, New Jersey: Prentice-Hall, 1968; Madison: Wisconsin Tales & Trails, 1973; and Madison: Northword, 1983 (in *Fire & Ice: Two Deadly Wisconsin Disasters*).

Wisconsin Assembly Journal, 1873. "Appendix," 157–231. (Lists of the dead, reports on relief efforts, and accounts of the fire.)

❧❧❧❧❧

Stephen J. Pyne is a professor at Arizona State University in Tempe and author of numerous books on wildland fire, including *Fire in America*.

The late **William Converse Haygood** served as editor of the *Wisconsin Magazine of History* from 1957 to 1975. He prepared this version of Father Pernin's account on the occasion of the Peshtigo Fire's centennial in 1971.